Hydroponics

Hydroponic Gardening: Growing Vegetables Without Soil

2nd Edition

Michael Hughston

Legal Notice:

Disclaimer Notice:

Table of Contents

Introduction

Thank you for downloading this book!

I hope that you find this introduction to hydroponic gardening to be useful as well as illuminating.

Growing plants without soil might sound like an idea that doesn't make much sense, but once you are exposed to the ideas behind why it works—it seems so easy.

This book will explain the basics of hydroponic gardening, which is a method of gardening that grows plants in water instead of soil, with an emphasis on at home applications. The substantial benefits of hydroponic growing are well worth the minuscule effort it takes to rise above the learning curve involved. Hydroponic gardening seems to have a mysterious aura about it which is often intimidating to the uninitiated. There are many persistent myths and misunderstandings surrounding the subject, which this book intends to dispel.

Contrary to popular opinion, a hydroponic set up need not be either expensive or complicated. After everything is said and done, you'll see for yourself that hydroponics is just as simple and straightforward as planting seeds in the ground. It might even be better!

Thanks again and I hope you enjoy reading this book!

Mike

Chapter One:
What Is Hydroponic Gardening?

Hydroponic gardening is a way to grow plants in water instead of soil, as is traditionally done. Everyone knows that the prefix "Hydro" refers to water. "Ponics" is a less modern Greek word meaning "work" or "labor." That makes "Hydroponic" a word that means "Water that does the work" sometimes translated as "Working water." This refers to the fact that water is used instead of soil.

Hydroponic growing methods offer several advantages over more traditional methods of growing food and has been steadily growing in popularity over recent years.

Typically, a seed draws the nutrients it needs to grow from the soil which is surrounding it. The minerals in the soil are used by the seed to start the growth process and allow it to begin growing. The seed reaches towards the surface and at the same time it also grows downward to establish a root system. The surrounding soil helps the plants roots stay securely in the ground.

Hydroponic gardening works because it is not really the soil that is necessary to make a seed grow into a plant, it is the minerals in the soil and the stability provided to the root system that really make the seed's growth possible. If these needs can be met in other ways, the seed will begin to grow in the absence of soil.

Growing plants hydroponically involves replacing the soil with a nutrient rich liquid solution. The solution can be tailored to match the nutritional needs and Ph preferences of the plants being grown, this catering to the specific needs of your crops often results in larger, healthier fruits and vegetables that are higher in nutritional content than their traditionally grown counterparts.

The roots of the plants are either suspended directly in the liquid nutrient solution or are allowed to grow in what is referred to as an "inert growing medium" usually this is some type of sand or clay-like material that can help the plant stabilize itself.

Many common varieties of vegetables can benefit from being grown hydroponically. Fruits and decorative plants are also well suited to this method of gardening. As mentioned, plants grown in this manner tend to be larger and of a higher nutritional content than ones grown in soil. This makes hydroponic gardening appealing to a wide range of gardening enthusiasts, from the backyard hobbyist all the way up to the off the grid homesteader and even large-scale commercial operations.

Whatever your level of gardening experience, there is a good chance you too, may benefit from this alternative way of growing your own food!

A Brief History of Hydroponic Gardening

Growing plants in water instead of soil is an ancient practice dating back to Babylon's hanging gardens. The Chinese also were using this method in antiquity; they were famous in the ancient world for their "Floating Gardens".

In the modern era, the process of soil-less growing was described by Francis Bacon in a book called "Sylva Sylvarum," published in 1627. This was among the first mentions made of soilless growing methods in European Scientific Literature. Between 1627 and the 1860's growing plants in water had become more sophisticated and somewhat demystified.

As scientists began to experiment with different ways of growing plants in water the techniques became more and more refined. It was discovered that the water could be mixed with nutrients in order to help the plants grow to a larger size than normal. These early attempts at understanding soilless growing methods were referred to as "Solution Culture." This term was commonly used as a blanket term for hydroponic gardening by the scientific community until the 1920's. Nowadays, the term "Solution Culture" is used to describe growing plants in a liquid without a grow material to stabilize the roots.

The hydroponic gardening we know today is based on these early efforts and continues to evolve and change as more research and experimentation takes place. Today, advances in technology have made it possible for nearly anyone to reap the rewards of soil-less growing.

Aside from bigger, more nutritious fruits and vegetables, what does hydroponic gardening offer the modern gardener?

The Advantages of Hydroponic Gardening

The reason plants grown hydroponically are often larger than their soil-grown counterparts has to do with the fact that absorbing nutrients through a liquid solution is much more efficient a process to the plant than it is with soil, the food is easier to digest, in a sense. Because of this ease of absorption hydroponic plants are usually upwards of fifty percent larger than soil grown plants! Some of the other advantages of hydroponic growing are:

- Crop yields are also significantly increased, and the nutritional content is often higher than the same plant grown in a more traditional manner.

Not only are you getting more fruits and vegetables with hydroponic gardening, you're getting larger and healthier ones too!

- Creating a garden is possible even in spaces where there is no soil. That means that you can grow plants in living spaces like condominiums and apartments. It also opens up the possibility of converting multi-level buildings into full-fledged agriculture patches.

- It allows you to grow food in places that are traditionally not fit for agriculture, such as arid areas. Israel and Arizona have long adopted this technique of growing crops, which allows their citizens to enjoy home-grown food and also to expand their food market. It also allows remote and unreachable places that have no agricultural space, such as Bermuda, to grow their own crops. Areas like Alaska and Russia that experience short seasons for planting has also adopted hydroponics and incorporated them in greenhouses so that they can have better control of climate for their plants.

- Maintaining your hydroponic setup is easier than taking care of a soil garden. They tend to use less water, which may sound counter-intuitive since the plants are being grown in water. However, in this setup, the water is always being reused.

- Maintaining proper Ph levels is also easier. So too, is ensuring that your crops get the proper nutrition they both need and deserve.

- Pests are also often less of a concern, and those that do find their way around are more easily dealt with.

- Harvesting crops is also often a simpler process when growing hydroponically.

When looking at the above advantages, you might be thinking, "Where's the catch?" There has to be a downside here right? Otherwise, hydroponic growing would be more widespread and commonplace. Hydroponics can seem complicated at first, the thick veil of technical jargon scares many people away before they have the chance to discover just how simple it can be to start growing plants hydroponically.

Chapter Two:
An Overview of Common Hydroponic Systems

There are many ways to go about setting up an at-home hydroponic garden. Which method you choose should be determined by how complicated a setup you're willing to deal with or capable of handling and what you wish to grow.

Before You Decide on a System

Before you start buying pre-made hydroponic systems or start setting up a DIY one, take into consideration the type of plants that you will be growing. You will need to take the following into consideration:

1. The size of the plant
2. The size of the roots
3. How the oxygen will reach the roots
4. How much water will the plants consume
5. The maximum amount of space you have for a hydroponic system
6. The nutrients that your plants will need in order to grow
7. How your plants will get light

No matter which type of plants you are planning to grow, you will definitely want to

Build and design a hydroponic system that you will use more than once. With this in mind, you should first think about how you are going to harvest the crops in the future and then clean the system for the next batch of crops that you are going to place in there. At the same time, you will also need to create a system that will give you the allowances that you need while your plants are still growing. That means that it should be able to give you the space that you need when it comes to fixing problems that might arise without damaging the plants that are already in them.

Take note that any type of hydroponic system can be used for growing most types of plants if you design it in such a way that it will accommodate all needs that you can think of, even when the crops reach their full size. However, you may find that some crops may require less maintenance and funds if you grow them in another type of system instead, rather than trying to grow all of the crops that you have in mind in one large system.

Hydroponic System Parts

These are the parts that you will need to have in order to build any type of hydroponic system:

1. Growing Chamber/Tray

    The growing chamber serves as the container of the plant roots. This is also that part of your hydroponic system that is dedicated to providing plant support, and also for the roots to have access to the nutrient solution. It also serves as the primary protection of the roots from heat, light, and pests.

    It is crucial to take note that your system should be able to keep the root zone away from light and heat. Prolonged exposure to light can cause damage to the roots, and the roots' exposure to high temperature will cause heat stress to the plants that you intend to grow. If your plants get stressed from heat, it will result in less flower or crop yield.

That means that you should choose a growing chamber that will meet this criterion. However, that is not to say that you should be restricting the type of material or design of the growing chamber to use for your hydroponic project. As long as the material does not corrode and can hold the root zone of your crops, then you can incorporate it into your system.

2.   Reservoir

The reservoir is the part that holds the nutrient solution. The nutrient solution is made up of all the nutrients that your plants need to grow that are dissolved in water. Depending on the system that you are going to choose, the nutrient solution should be pumped into the reservoir in such a way that the solution will reach the growing chamber in specific cycles, or continually if the crop of your choice requires it. In some designs, the reservoir may also serve as the growing chamber as well, if the plant needs to have its roots touching the reservoir all the time.

If you are choosing to DIY, you can create a reservoir by using a clean plastic container that can hold water and is light proof. By ensuring that no light can pass through the reservoir and cleaning it thoroughly, you can be sure that there will be no algae and other microorganisms that will grow in it and cause damage to your plants.

3.   Submersible pump

This pump is required in all systems to deliver the nutrient solution from the reservoir to the growing chamber. You can easily find these pumps in most home improvement stores that sell fountain, pond, or garden supplies. The size of the pump will depend on the amount of water that you need to pump into your hydroponic system, which is measured by gallons per hour (gph).

Ideally, you will get a pump that will deliver twice the minimum gph that your plants require in order to give you an allowance for flexibility once your plants grow. It should also allow you to fit it with a filter or a screen to make cleaning easier.

4.   Delivery system

The delivery system serves as the plumbing system that allows the pump to deliver the nutrient solution from the reservoir to the growing chamber, and then back to the reservoir. You can use virtually any kind of material for this, such as standard PVC pipes, garden connectors, and irrigation tubes, or vinyl tubing. So long as it will not corrode, you may use it.

If you are trying to use drip or aeroponic system, you may want to make sure that the delivery system that you will be using will be a spray or drip emitter.

However, keep in mind that delivery systems for drip and aeroponics may clog, so you may want to have spare ones for easy swapping.

5.   Timer

You may need at least two timers for your hydroponic system if you are going to use artificial lighting instead of sunlight. If you are going to use drip, flood and drain, or aeroponic system, you will need to set off a timer to control the cut-off times of the pump.

6.   Air pump

Air pumps are optional in hydroponics, but you may want to have them anyway since they are inexpensive and can be easily purchased at any store that sells aquariums. Their main purpose is to supply oxygen to the growing chamber by creating bubbles that pass through the nutrient solution.

Air pumps can be very useful if you are using water culture systems since they can prevent the plants from suffocated when their roots are submerged in the solution all the time. For other hydroponic systems, air pumps can be useful in making sure that the plant nutrients are evenly mixed in the nutrient solution by circulating the water and the nutrients in the solution. Circulating water will also prevent stagnation in the reservoir, which may cause pathogen growth.

7.   Grow lights

Grow lights are another optional component in a hydroponic system. Compared to standard house lights, grow lights emit color spectrums that mimic natural sunlight, which is necessary to encourage photosynthesis. These lights are typically used when the location of a hydroponic system does not have adequate natural lighting.

Now that you have an idea of what hydroponic systems are, you will be able to mix and match these components depending on how you plan to grow your plants. Keep in mind that you do not have to buy expensive hydroponic parts to successfully grow plants – in fact, you have the liberty to improvise what you are going to use. You will find out how you can create your first hydroponic system using DIY and cost-effective materials in the next chapter.

Five Common Types of Hydroponic Setups

Aeroponics

This method doesn't use a substrate or growing medium. Instead, plants are suspended in the air by using baskets or foam cell plugs (usually plugged into small holes at the upper portion of the growing chamber) that are compressed around the stem of the plants. A liquid solution is stored in the reservoir and the plants are misted with a nutrient solution at regular intervals. This type of hydroponic growing is used more in large commercial applications and is not very popular for at-home use. This system was developed as a way to reduce the amount of water used in growing crops to as small amount as possible.

Among the major factors that differentiate this hydroponic system from other setups is the water droplet size. In this system, the finer the nutrient solution sprayed to the plant roots, the faster the growth of the plants will be. For this reason, the plant canopy that you are looking to build will grow faster as well. If you are looking to create large-scale hydroponic systems, then this may be the hydroponic system that you will want to master.

When building an aeroponic system, you will need to have the following:

1. Submersible pump
2. Tubing for distributing the water from the reservoir pump to the misting or sprinkling heads in the growing chamber.

3.   A closed growing chamber that is airtight enough to prevent water from spilling out and to keep pests out, but will also allow fresh oxygen to reach the roots.

4.   Water tight container within the growing chamber

5.   A cycle timer to turn on and off the pump

6.   Tubing for returning the excess solution back to the reservoir

7.   Sprinkler or misting heads

Drip System

The drip system involves placing plants in a long tray or halved pipe and the nutrient solution drips from a basin into the tray, saturating the plant and providing it with what it needs to grow.

Ebb and Flow

The Ebb and Flow method works almost like the Drip method. Plants are placed in trays and stabilized with a growth medium. The area is flooded with a nutrient solution at regular intervals. The solution is pumped into the grow area and allowed to circulate through the plants and is then pumped out.

This system is very popular because it is very easy to build and that you can use almost any material that you have lying around in your home to create a hydroponic system. At the same time, most ebb and flow systems can fit any space that you have, whether it is indoors or outdoors.

You will need the following when building an ebb-and-flow system:

1.   A submersible pump

2.   A timer that will turn the pump on and off

3.   Any tubing that will allow the water to run from the pump as it drains the water from the reservoir to flood the growth chamber

4.   A tube that will set the height for the water level when the solution is pumped to the growth chamber

5.   Any container that will serve as reservoir

6.   A container that will serve as the growing medium.

Always remember that you need to make sure that there is a way for air to get to the top of the overflow and prevent the water solution from spilling out of your growth chamber. You can make a T connector that extends a little above the line. By having this connector running from the bottom of the growth chamber, you can be ensured that there will be air pockets in your system and allow the water to flood and drain the chamber without trouble.

Also, see to it that your overflow tube is larger than the inlet tube of your pump; otherwise, the water that you are pumping in will be more than what goes out of the overflow tube. This will cause the water to spill out from the top of your system unless you reduce the volume pressure from the pump.

Nutrient Film Technique (NFT)

When using the Nutrient Film Technique, the roots of the plants you are growing are submerged directly into the water solution. The plants float around the tank in plastic baskets as they absorb the nutrient solution, which is continuously being pumped through the tank. This is among the more simple and direct methods of hydroponic gardening but is not suitable for plants that are easily waterlogged.

This system is ideal for home DIY hydroponic growers because of its simple design but is mainly ideal for growing small crops that grow quickly. If you are looking to build this system, you will need the following:

1. Any container that will hold the nutrient solution, or a reservoir

2. A submersible pump

3. Any form of tubing that will allow the water to flow from the pump to the growing tub

4. A gully or a channel that will serve as growing tubes for the plants

5. A channel that allows the used nutrient solution to the reservoir.

Most commercial users of the NFT system typically use specialized channels that have flat bottoms that are fitted with grooves that run along the entire channel. The grooves make it possible to allow the water to flow along the suspended roots and prevent the channel from accumulating too much water. For DIY home growers, vinyl rain gutters are a popular choice, since they also have these similar grooves, but costs less than the special commercial gullies.

If there is a quick downside to building an NFT system as your first hydroponic system, it is that they are very vulnerable to unforeseen and sudden interruptions when it comes to the flow of water. Plants are very aware of interruptions in the flow of nutrients, which may cause quick wilting for some crops.

Wick System

The wick system is an excellent choice for those just starting out with at home hydroponic gardening. It doesn't entail using anything with moving parts–there are no complicated growing sets up to be concerned with. However, you will need a pump.

Because there are no moving parts, this is referred to as being a "passive" form of hydroponic growing. Passive systems are a good choice for those starting out because they are easy to maintain–a lack of moving parts also mean a lack of things that can break down. They are also more inexpensive to get started with and maintain. The drawbacks to using a passive system are that they are not well suited to high maintenance fruits and vegetables or to those plants that require large quantities of water. That means that if you intend to plant crops like peppers, tomatoes, and most fruit-bearing plants, you may want to select another type of system since they require heavy feeding. Wick systems are also poor at making you certain that you are feeding your plants with equal ratios of nutrients since it does not spread out the nutrient solution evenly. It can be a very possible scenario that your plants will just absorb the water that is present in the wick, along with the nutrients that come along with it. The rest of the unused nutrients will be left sitting in the nutrient solution in the reservoir, which can turn into a toxic composition for plants. For that reason, never use the remaining solution at the bottom of the wick system for other systems that you may have at home. Also, make it a point that you flush out the excess minerals that will be sitting at the bottom of your crop's root zone with fresh water at least once a week.

When using the wick system, the plants are suspended in a growth medium, usually coconut fiber or vermiculite, and then placed in a grow tray, which is filled with water.

Underneath the grow tray is another tank, called the reservoir. This component contains a pump and is connected to the grow tray by wicks.

The wicks transfer the nutrient solution in the reservoir to the grow tray, where it is absorbed by the plants roots.

Growing Mediums

Growing mediums are inert materials that the plants are placed in; they fulfill the root stabilizing function traditionally provided by soil. They are also called "Substrates." A grow medium is often made from naturally occurring substances such as clay, gravel or plant husks but using man-made materials, such as plastic and Styrofoam are pretty common choices as well.

Growing mediums, compared to soil, are not capable of growing plants on their own. That means that if you place plants in them and use plain water, the plants will starve out because of nutrient deficiency. For that reason, you can consider growing mediums as the part of the system that supports the weight of the plants and the vessel that maintains moisture and oxygen that crops need in order to grow. The nutrient solution ensures that the plants are properly nourished.

While you can use almost anything to serve as a growing medium, it is crucial that you choose materials that go along the design of your hydroponic system. That means that in

every hydroponic system, there is an ideal type of growing medium to use. Take a look at them here:

1. Drip system – you will need to use a growing medium that will allow proper drainage and limit the amount of water that pools inside it. For this reason, most experienced DIY hydroponic system builders use river rocks at the bottom to assist in drainage and prevent the growing media from keeping a pool of water at the bottom.

2. Flood and drain systems – this system will allow a variety of growing medium designs, as long as you do not use any material that floats on water, such as Vermiculite and Perlite. This is because when the system cycles and the solution is drained out, the growing media may tilt or become out of balance, causing the plants to lose all the support that they have and may tilt over because of gravity. What you can do is to lower the flood level so that the plants still keep in contact with the remaining

moisture and maintain support. However, if you are growing vine-type plants such as melons or tomatoes, you can tie them up in trellis instead.

You also want to choose a support medium that allows good drainage, so you may want to add river rocks at the bottom of the system as well. This way, you can avoid pooling of water at the bottom. If river rocks are unavailable, you can use coco chips as an inexpensive alternative.

3.   NFT systems – these systems are shallow, but they require a steady stream of water. For this reason, ideal growing mediums will be starter cubes or small baskets (about 1 inch). Make sure that your growing mediums are not too close to the water supply, since they may become water saturated and lead to stem rot.

4.   Water culture systems – these systems do not require as much growing media since the plants will be required to submerge their roots to the nutrient solutions. The ideal medium is a starter basket that is installed a little above the nutrient solution. This way, the basket won't not be water-saturated but can maintain moisture at the bottom. Since the top of the basket is dry, the roots will naturally grow downward and reach the nutrient solution.

5.   Wick systems – these are the most uncommon hydroponic systems, but they are ideal for

those who do not want to rely on pumps, motors, or any moving parts. With a wick system, you want to use a growing media that can absorb and hold the moisture. If you want to control the amount of solution in the wick, you can use multiple fabrics so that you can easily adjust the amount of moisture.

6. Aeroponic systems – these systems do not really require growing media, so consider getting ones that allow the roots to hang in the air as they get misted with nutrient solution. That means that you want to start the crop seeds in a starter cube, and then move them into larger ones when they are big enough to avoid root suffocation. Also, make sure that the growing mediums that you are going to use are installed in such a way that they won't not be waterlogged to prevent rotting.

Some commonly used grow mediums are:

- Coconut husks
- Wool
- Packing peanuts
- Sand
- Gravel
- Clay
- Pumice
- Vermiculite

These are not the only choices, just those that are most commonly used and preferred by a majority of hydroponic gardeners.

Nutrient Solutions

When it comes to choosing a nutrient solution, your best bet is to purchase one of the many commercially available formulas that have been designed specifically for the plants you intend to grow. However, keep in mind that hydroponic solutions can be costly in the long run since they may range from $.30 per gallon upwards. While there are cost-effective nutrient solution manufacturers, it is imperative that you learn how to mix your own if you intend to produce crops in a long-term and large-scale basis.

It is possible to mix up a batch of homemade nutrient solution on your own, but this adds an unnecessary complication to the entire process and is not recommended for those with little or no experience. If you want to mix your own nutrient solution, use the following guide:

1. If you are going to use a fertilizer, make sure that it is soluble in water. Check for the concentration. Since you have the ability to immediately monitor your solution, you can make sure that you are achieving relative consistency. All you need is to have a nutrient meter.

2. All the other elements that you need for growing your crops in a hydroponic solution (apart from oxygen, carbon, and hydrogen

that can be absorbed from air and water) will come from mineral nutrients. A great hydroponic solution should have the following minerals in correct ratios:

a. Nitrogen (N)

b. Phosphorous (P)

c. Potassium (K)

d. Copper (Cu)

e. Zinc (Zn)

f. Iron (Fe)

g. Sulfur (S)

h. Manganese (Mn)

i. Molybdenum (Mo)

j. Magnesium (Mg)

k. Chlorine (Cl)

l. Boron (B)

m. Calcium (Ca)

If you are worried about ratios, you can check how these elements are incorporated in commercial hydroponic nutrients. You will also see that these pre-made solutions come in different "parts" formulation, depending on what a DIY hydroponic grower prefers for his crops. Since you are starting out, you can choose to stick to general instructions for ratios before you experiment.

Make sure that the nutrients that you are going to use for your hydroponic system are created for hydroponic use. That means that the nutrients that you should purchase for your DIY mix should be designed for water, instead of soil, since soil nutrient mixes are very different when they are dissolved in water. Here's an example: Nitrogen for soil more often comes in the form of urea, but it is not suitable for hydroponics since urea is not water soluble. In order to add Nitrogen to your hydroponic solution, you will need to use Nitrate instead.

Make sure that your nutrients are stored and added using the right temperature. Keep in mind that roots of most plants grow underground and to duplicate that effect, you need to keep the root zone temperature at 68-72 Fahrenheit. While it does not mean that a slight elevation of temperature will kill the crops that you intend to grow, you should still make sure that the root temperature stays close to the above-mentioned temperature range. If the nutrients are stored at a higher temperature than advised, it can result in damaged fruits, no new growth, or flowers falling off or turning to yellow.

Chapter Three:
A Simple At Home Hydroponic setup For Beginners

You can set up your hydroponic grow system indoors, outdoors or in a backyard greenhouse. When growing indoors you will need to replicate artificially the environmental conditions that enable plants to grow.

These conditions are:

- Proper Nutrients–provided by your liquid solution.

- Water -usually supplied by the gardener or rainfall. In Hydroponic growing, water is what plants are grown in so you'll have no issue providing water to your plants.

- A way to stabilize the root system which is provided by the grow medium.

- Sunlight which is provided by access to windows or grow lights.

- The temperature which can easily be artificially controlled in most buildings.

As long as the needs of the plant can be met adequately, they will grow just fine no matter if they are in soil or a nutrient solution.

We took a look at five common hydroponic systems that are currently being used. Each offered a different way of growing plants without soil but might still seem a little too complex for those just starting out.

The method we will now consider is called the water culture method and is relatively easy to construct and perfect for the first timer.

To set up your own at home water culture grow system you will need:

An aquarium or other suitable water tight container. It is important that your container be opaque- no light should be able to get through it. Light helps out the growth of algae, which can cause you and your plants a multitude of problems. If your tank is not light proof, then you will either need to paint it black or cover it with something that is light proof.

Make sure you leave an inch or two of unpainted surface near the top of the container to be able to see how much water is in it. This step is optional but will make things easier for you down the line.

You will also need a sheet of Styrofoam. To obtain one that is the proper size, measure the length and width of your tank and subtract about a 1/4 or so. For example, say your tank is 12 inches wide and 36 inches long. You'll want your Styrofoam sheet to be 11 3/4 inches by 35 3/4 inches.

You will need to cut some more holes in the sheet in a bit so it can accommodate your net pots. Don't go placing it in the fish tank just yet, set it aside for now.

A pump is needed to ensure the water maintains Oxygen levels sufficient enough to keep your plants alive. The exact type of pump you will need is going to be determined by how many gallons of water your tank can hold. Be sure to check the package or seek the advice of those who have more experience. The pump will be placed in the reservoir tank.

Make sure you have enough net pots and growing medium for the amount of plants you intend to grow. Net pots are made of plastic and are netted to allow water to circulate through them.

The number of plants you are able to fit in your tank is going to depend on just how big your tank is and the size of your plants. Make sure that each plant has a little space of its own and that access to light isn't blocked.

Don't forget to get a nutrient solution that is suitable for what you intend to grow.

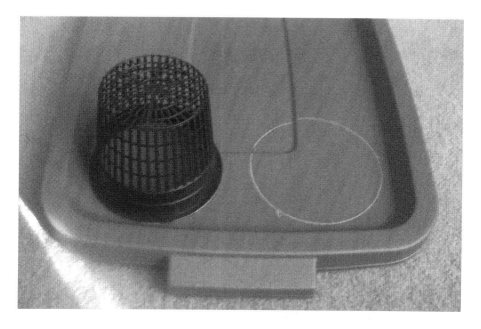

Setting Up Your Water Culture System

Before you start, make sure your Styrofoam sheet is the correct size. It should fit in the reservoir and be free to rise and fall with the water level.

Once you have determined that the sheet is of the correct size, you want to cut a hole for each net pot you intend to use. Simply trace the bottom of the net pot onto the Styrofoam sheet and cut it out. You'll also want to cut a hole or notch for your filter's airline, so go ahead and do that.

The first thing to do is fill the reservoir with nutrient solution and place your plants in the net pots, making sure they are being held in place by the grow medium.

After the preparation of your tank and plants has been accomplished, it's time to set up your pump. Place the Styrofoam on the tank and place the air tube through the notch or hole you have made. Now all that remains is to put your potted plants in their respective holes and turn on your pump.

Congratulations! You are now a proud owner of a functional home hydroponic growing system. Now begins the familiar routine of caring for your plants and giving them the attention they need to provide you with a bounty of delicious and nutritious food for you and your family.

This simple set up is perfect for growing lettuce and other leafy green vegetables in addition to many common herbs. It's not the most efficient hydroponic system available, its simplicity and minimal maintenance requirements make it an excellent first step into the world of hydroponic growing.

Chapter Four:
What Can Your Grow?

If you are thinking of adapting hydroponics in your household to expand your food list, or to reduce the cost of your grocery expenses, then it makes sense that you also take into consideration of what you can actually grow in the absence of actual soil. When you consider that plants do not require much to grow, you begin to realize that you can virtually grow anything through hydroponics.

Many popular fruits, vegetables, and herbs can be grown in your (or someone else's) hydroponic gardening system. The choices listed below are just the tip of the iceberg. Just about anything that will grow in your local area in the soil can be grown hydroponically. Some of the more popular and common choices are:

Fruits

Cantaloupe (Cucumis melo)

Sometimes called "Rock-melons," Cantaloupes are a roundish, orange-fleshed type of melon which currently holds the honor of being America's most popular melon.

These melons have been being cultivated by humans for over four thousand years. Like just about all fruits, they are high in Vitamin C. They also contain plenty of Manganese and beta carotene.

Raspberries (Rubus idaeus, Rubus occidentalis, Rubus, etc.)

There are many different types of Raspberry; they are all members of the Rose family. Raspberries are used in a variety of culinary applications and are often made into jellies, jams and used as a pie filling.

These berries are high in dietary fiber and Vitamin C. They also are a good source of manganese and Vitamin K. Aside from the berry the leaves of this plant are also used to prepare tea.

Many varieties of Raspberry are easy to grow, so easy that they may border on becoming invasive. This is an excellent choice for any hydroponic setup.

Strawberries (Fragaria ananassa)

The strawberry is technically not a berry. It is what is called an "aggregate accessory fruit," which is a fruit which consists of several of a flower's ovaries combining into a single unit. The "seeds" seen on a strawberry are really individual ovaries with an actual seed inside them.

The Strawberry is one of the most popular fruits in the entire world and has been so for thousands of years. It's reputation as a delicious addition to a variety of desserts stretches back to ancient Rome.

Strawberries provide a decent amount of Manganese and Vitamin C and may provide some protection against heart disease.

Strawberries do very well in most hydroponic gardens and are a popular choice among many gardeners.

Watermelon (Citrullus Lantus)

This common North American melon originated in South Africa and has been being grown consumed by humans since prehistory. By the 1700s, watermelons were a common sight in gardens the word over.

The entire watermelon is edible, rind seeds and all. Most often the rind and seeds are discarded, this is a shame. The seeds can be roasted and enjoyed like sunflower seeds and the rind is sometimes pickled or used in salads.

The average watermelon is high in vitamin C and is over 90% water.

Vegetables

Cucumbers (Cucumis sativus)

This vine growing dietary staple needs no introduction. The cucumber has many uses and is easy to grow using hydroponic techniques. This vegetable is just as popular fresh as it is pickled. The cucumber is a little lacking in the nutrition department when compared to the other vegetables on this list. It does offer a moderate amount of Vitamin K and is comprised of over 95% water.

Lettuce (Lactuca sativa)

Lettuce is an excellent candidate for your hydroponic garden; it grows easily, has many uses and, depending on which variety you are growing can be a fairly nutritious addition to your diet. The humble head of lettuce contains high levels of vitamin A, beta-carotene and almost an entire day's worth of Vitamin K.

Peas (Pisum sativum)

Peas are technically a fruit, like tomatoes. There are many varieties of peas. The most common and familiar is the green pea.They tend to grow well in a hydroponic manner and are recommended for beginners.

Peas offer a pretty impressive group of nutrients, including high amounts of vitamin C, vitamin K, Vitamins B5 and B6, vitamin A, dietary fiber. In addition to vitamins and fiber peas are full of minerals such as zinc, copper, lutein, and magnesium. They are also high in sugar, making them an excellent source of energy.

Spinach (Spinacia oleracea)

Spinach, most popular as Popeye's favorite food, was first cultivated in ancient Persia. It became known in Europe sometime during the ninth century and became a popular dietary staple in the 1500s.

In modern times, spinach has always been valued and praised as an incredibly nutritious plant. Its high iron content alone is enough to justify this reputation, but spinach has much more to offer. An excellent source of Calcium, B complex vitamins, Vitamin A, Magnesium, Manganese, Potassium, and Zinc. A single serving of spinach contains nearly four times the daily requirement of vitamin K. All things considered, fresh spinach is a worthwhile addition to anyone's diet as well as being a great plant to grow hydroponically.

Tomatoes (Solanum Lycopersicum)

Oddly enough tomatoes had a rough time making their way into the human diet. They were considered by many ancient peoples to be poisonous, some cultures thought eating them would turn one into a werewolf. Eventually, it was figured out that this was not the case, and people began to see how very useful tomatoes can be in the kitchen.

Tomatoes are a popular choice for both traditional and hydroponic gardens and with good reason. They grow easily, offer a high yield and have many culinary applications. Nutritionally speaking they are an excellent source of antioxidants—compounds which are suspected of having disease-fighting properties. They are high in vitamin C and a great source of trace minerals.

Herbs

Basil (Ocimum basilicum)

Basil is a very common cooking herb with a myriad of uses. It's a member of the mint family. This herb loves growing in warm sunny climates but does just fine indoors as well. It's a well know repellent of insects and other pests and will help keep them out of

your garden, which makes it worth growing for that reason alone.

Dill (Anethum graveolens)

Both the seeds and the leaves of this herb are edible and useful in the kitchen. The leaves are often referred to as "dill weed" and are used to enhance the flavor of many dishes, from soups to roasted meats. Dill weed is used in a similar fashion as Parsley.

Dill seed is often crushed and used as a spice. The seeds are similar in taste to caraway seeds and are used in the same way. Dill seeds are most well known for adding their distinctive flavor to dill pickles.

Dill likes as much sunlight as it can get, even partial shade can inhibit its growth. It is also known to attract helpful insects that prey on more invasive and destructive pests.

Mint

There are many types of mint that are commonly grown in gardens. Mint is one of the world's most popular flavoring agents and is used nearly everywhere–cooking, candies, desserts, gum, etc..

This hardy perennial herb is commonly found growing near water. They also prefer shade to full on sunlight and enjoy cool, moist spots as a general rule. This doesn't mean your mint won't grow well under different conditions–it will, don't worry about that.

Many gardeners find that mint grows a little too well, left unchecked it will happily take over all of your available garden space. Make sure to keep a watchful eye on any mint you have growing. Just one or two plants are usually enough to provide you with all the mint you could ever use. It is common practice to plant mint as a means to keep pests at bay and to attract beneficial insects.

Mint is best used fresh, harvested right before it is going to used.

Oregano (Origanum vulgare)

This purple flowered ubiquitous cooking herb is a relative of Marjoram and is sometimes called "Wild Marjoram."

Oregano favors hot and somewhat dry conditions but does well most anywhere.

The leaves of the Oregano plant are often dried and used as a popular addition to many standard Italian-American dishes. Many types of Middle Eastern cuisine also make heavy use of this herb, using it to flavor beef and mutton in addition to using it as a condiment, in the same way many people use salt and pepper.

Rosemary (Rosmarinus officinalis)

Another member of the mint family, Rosemary is grown by gardeners the world over both as a decoration and for use in cooking.The leaves are commonly dried first and used to add flavor to roasted meats and various types of stuffing. Fresh leaves are sometimes used to make a tea. It is also a primary ingredient in some types of vinegar. The essential oil is popularly used as an ingredient in perfumes.

It is easily waterlogged and unsuitable for hydroponic methods that involve leaving the roots of the plants suspended in water all the time. Like just most all the members of the Mint family, Rosemary is sometimes used as a form of natural pest control.

This brief list is just a small introduction to what it is possible for you to grow. A little digging will reveal a list of plants that are due to do well in your particular climate.

Chapter Five:
Expanding Your Farm

At this point, you probably have a better idea of what you intend to grow in your hydroponic garden. Since you are not limited by the availability of soil in your location, you can now take the opportunity to grow more plants and expanding your crop list by incorporating the right hydroponic system for each plant that you intend to grow.

Some Precautions

Before you decide for a crop lock in, consider what the immediate future will look like for the plants that you intend to grow in your hydroponic garden. Keep in mind that as plants grow, they form more mature roots, which prompt you to adjust the space that your crops will occupy. They also begin to require more nutrients and sunlight to ensure proper and healthy growth.

This means that as your crops mature, you need to make adjustments in your DIY garden. To ensure that your hydroponic system will be able to contain the plants that it holds and that they progress into healthy mature crops, keep these general rules in mind:

1. For small plants, maintain a minimum water volume of ½ gallons per plant

2.   For medium-sized plants, maintain a minimum water volume or 1 to ½ gallons per plant

3.   For large plants, maintain a minimum water volume of 2 ½ gallons per plant.

How Big Can Your System Get?

There are different conditions that may affect the amount of nutrients and water that your plants can take as they grow. At this point, you may want to consider upgrading the size of your hydroponic system and consider doubling the minimum water volume requirement as you start planting. Why should you opt to do this, instead of keeping a small DIY system that will fit snugly in your space? It is because plants that grow in a hydroponic system tend to grow faster, which means that it can be quite a hassle to transfer all of your crops to a bigger system in the middle of the grow. Making a transfer before your harvest can also cause some logistical problems and it also costs more money, too.

Should You Grow Different Plants in One System?

If you have had the chance to make a garden before, you know that it is possible for you to plant different crops in a single garden patch without having much trouble. Now, can you plant different crops in a single hydroponic system?

Yes, it may be possible for you to plant similar crops in a single system; however, you may want to think twice about doing so. Not only will you want to avoid crowding the growth chamber, you should also remember that different types of plants have different nutrient and pH requirement. The pH requirement of each plant dictates how well the nutrients pass through the root cells. If the pH of the nutrient solution is out of balance for another type of crop that is in the same system, it may cause this crop to starve and eventually wilt.

To be safe, make sure that you place a different type of crop in another hydroponic system. If you are using the same hydroponic solution for another set of plants, you should see to it that the pH solution of the remaining solution meets the demands of your new plants and the nutrient solution left in the reservoir is enough to feed the plants that you grow in the system. If you are unsure about the remaining elements in the reservoir and you have the slightest doubt when it comes to the toxicity of the solution, do not use the leftover nutrient solution anymore and mix a new batch.

Some Notes When Measuring and Altering pH

If you are proceeding with mixing larger batches of nutrient solutions for bigger crops and hydroponic systems, then you need to see to it that you are measuring the pH of the nutrient solutions that you are producing. The best way to do it is to test the pH with the nutrients already in the water to make sure that you are getting the true reading. You can purchase a pH testing kit for under $10 to check for acidity and alkaline content of your mix.

However, there will be occasions when you need to test the pH balance of the nutrient solution in your reservoirs more frequently, especially if you notice some abnormalities in your plants. If that is the case, the best way to ensure that you are getting true pH readings while troubleshooting is to get a pH testing meter. They may cost a little under $100, but it is definitely worth the investment.

If you need to adjust the pH of your nutrient mix, then you may also opt to get pH adjusters, instead of manually altering the elements that you are placing in your solution. Remember that too much of an element may cause toxicity in your nutrient solution, making an entire batch unfit to use to nourish your plants. PH adjusters usually come in either liquid or dry form, but they are water soluble. To use them, simply use the pH down formula to adjust a higher pH than recommended, and the pH up for lower pH.

Chapter Six:
Hydroponics and Water

Water is among the most essential elements that your crops need, and for that reason, you need to pay special attention to it. In this chapter, you will learn how to make sure that you are using the right kind and amount of water for your plants.

When to Water Plants

Since you are dealing with a process of growing plants without soil, you may be wondering if you should water your plants at all. The answer is a resounding "yes;" you need to still water your plants.

However, there is no straightforward answer when it comes to how often you should water your plants. It depends on the following factors:

1. Water temperature
2. Type of growing medium
3. Type of crop
4. Size of plants
5. Humidity
6. Air temperature

You may, on the other hand, try to keep this goal in mind when it comes to watering your plants: you need to water your plants to make sure that the roots and the growing medium is wet. However, you need to prevent the roots from suffocating because there is not much oxygen around them anymore. Your goal is also to make sure that the plants do not dry out. That means that if you see any signs of wilting, the first thing that you need to check is if you are watering your plants too little or too much.

The reason that you need to water your plants, even while using a hydroponic system, is relatively simple – you need the roots to maintain enough moisture so that they can have enough water content to support foliage. The amount of moisture that the roots can hold and absorb depend on how much they need water – plants in dry temperature want to absorb more than those that are in humid conditions. There are also plants that are planted in a growing medium that keeps better moisture than the others, thus requiring less watering.

When watering plants, you may make it a point to maintain a schedule of watering your hydroponic plants. For some crops, you may opt to water them for 30 minutes, depending on the growth medium that you are using. You also try using a timer to determine the best times when you should be watering your plants and adjust your watering schedule. Watering at night may not be necessary since plants tend to only absorb water when light is available. However, if your aim is to keep the growing medium moist, then you can water the plants when the lights are off.

Woes About Water Quality

Most growers do not pay much attention to the quality of water that they are using in their hydroponic system reservoir and for watering their plants. If you have been drinking water from the tap and you are sure that it is sparkling clear, you may think that it is also safe for your plants. However, you need to think twice about doing that – the water that people drink is not pure H2O, but also a combination of mineral deposits, dissolved gasses, pathogens, chemicals, and dust.

While there are many water-soluble substances that may be present in the local tap water that your plants may use, like manganese and calcium, there are also substances that may be dangerous for your plants. Some pathogens available in tap water are not dangerous to human beings at all, but may wreak havoc on your hydroponic system.

How to Test the Water

If you are intending to grow plants indoors and you are planning to use tap water to water your plants, you should first know what can be found in that type of water. You can ask for a complete report from your municipality for analysis. If your water comes from other supplies, such as dams, rivers, or underground, you may want to send a sample water to the lab for analysis.

Take note that water analysis reports may not cover all the things that you need to know about all possible potential dangers when used on plants, it will be able to tell you all of the major water concerns that you need to know. Once you are sure what your water supply is made of, you can make the decision whether you can use it for your system or not.

What is the Best Water to Use?

If you do not have time to have your water supply tested, then make sure that you save yourself from a lot of trouble by using quality filtered water from the start. Take into consideration too that while water filtered through water softener systems are considered safe to drink since they are pathogen and bacteria-free, it may still contain traces of salt that can be toxic to your plants. Of course, there are certain plants are capable of tolerating salt, but repeated use of the same water will cause salt build up in your reservoir.

If possible, use RO water for your hydroponic system. If you do not have this water filtration system at home, you can make use of any good water filtration system that has these three filters:

1.   sediment filter

2.   activated charcoal filter

3.   0.5 microns filter, or absolute one-micron filter

Chapter Seven:
Lighting Your Hydroponics

If you are growing plants indoors, there is a big chance that they will not receive the light they need to photosynthesize. Without light, your plant will not be able to process the nutrients that you have been feeding it, causing it to starve itself. Of course, not everyone has access to a bright greenhouse or a patio, but that should not stop you from growing your choice of plants in the space that you have available at home.

Growing plants indoors should not be a problem as long as you are able to provide artificial lighting. With artificial lighting, you can replicate the warmth that plants receive from the sun, as well as the colors of the spectrum that it needs to proceed to photosynthesis. Use this chapter as a guide to installing artificial lighting in the room where you will be placing your hydroponic system.

The Rules to Lighting

Think about the lighting cycle that plants receive in their natural environment; a typical vegetable garden receives 8 to 10 hours of bright light outdoors, and at least 4 to 6 hours of direct sunlight. If you are going to move this vegetable garden indoors, you should be able to replicate these conditions. That means that you need to have 14 to 16 hours of bright lighting for your plants, and then 8 to 10 hours of darkness in order for your plants to have their much-needed rest and to aid their metabolism.

Since you are growing your plants in a controlled environment indoors, you have the liberty to use the artificial lighting that is best suited for the type of plants that you intend to grow. Below is the list of artificial lighting commonly used by hydroponic growers.

1.   Metal Halide Lights

These lights are preferred by many indoor growers over the rest of the available choices because they have better spectral distribution. That means that the bulbs are able to replicate bright sunlight, along with the energy wavelengths of a visible spectrum. Because these bulbs make your plants experience quality, sunlight-like energy, your plants are guaranteed to enjoy photosynthesis when you leave these lights on. By using these lights, you can ensure that your plants achieve the best possible height and flower growth. They are also best to use for a room that contains multiple crop types, as well as for growing multi-seasonal plants.

Metal halide bulbs also have long life and they do not tend to reduce luminosity over time. However, it does not mean that you should not replace them over time – if you are using these bulbs continuously at 18 hours per day for 12 months, they will only be giving out 85% of the brightness that your plants need.

2.   High Pressure Sodium Lights (HPS)

These lights come close to the metal halide grow lights when it comes to spectral distribution. They are capable of providing high yellow and red colors with the light that they emit, which is favorable to flower and fruit-bearing plants. These lights also have longer life expectancy, since they can last for up to 48 months.

3.   High Output Fluorescent Lights (T5 lights)

These lights look like a bunch of fluorescent tubes that are placed under a metal hood. They are the best lights to use when you are growing seedlings or encouraging clones to grow their own roots, thanks to the little heat that it produces.

These grow lights are capable of producing 5000 lumens per bulb and do not produce much heat compared to stronger grow lights like HPS. If you are growing in a small room, then these might be a good choice of grow lights for you since they also consume less electricity.

4.   LED Grow Lights

LED is becoming the new alternative for the sun without having the overhead cost of HPS or metal halide bulbs. They also produce less heat and consume less electricity, which makes them ideal for hydroponic growers that are trying to minimize overhead costs of growing crops. LED costs only ¼ of the energy consumption of a 400-watt HPS, and since it produces minimal heat, it can save you the cost of having to cool down your hydroponics system.

Using LED lights will make the plants grow shorter, stocky, and strong. You can also expect them to look a little different – the leaves tend to curl down a little, but they will be thicker and healthier-looking. You can also expect to have slower vegetation compared to when using 400 watts of HPS lighting, but the plants will still progress to be healthy and normal.

If you are growing fruit-bearing and flowering plants, you can also expect them to create yields slower than other plants that enjoy HPS and metal halide lighting. However, the fruits and flowers that an LED-lit plant will yield will have denser development, and their color will be more realistic. However, these lights are not recommended for growing big plants or multiple crops in a single room. It is more suited for growing a heat-free hobby garden.

5.   Compact Fluorescent Lights (CFLs)

CFLs are probably the beginner's small hydroponic system builder's best friend. They emit little to no heat, and they consume little electricity, making them ideal to use for hydroponic startup projects. If you are growing flowering or fruit-bearing plants, then choosing the 2700K warm light bulb is the best option. If you intend to grow plants that will grow taller than a foot, then you may use regular fluorescent lights on the plant sides to aid with lighting.

Take note that when you are using CFLs, you need to purchase the bulbs with the actual wattage on your mind, not their equivalent, when you are calculating how much energy you need to light up your hydroponic system.

Chapter Eight:
Some Problems You Might Encounter

Any type of garden or farm comes with its own set of problems, even hydroponic systems. In this chapter, you will learn about the most common nuisances that may exist when you are trying to grow crops in hydroponic systems and how to deal with them.

Make sure that you bookmark this chapter as it will serve as your troubleshooting guide for your first hydroponic system.

Rust-Like Spots On The Leaves Of Crops

These spots can be caused by one or more of the following:

1. Sapsuckers (bugs) – take a look at the leaf tops and undersides to see if there are any bugs. The reason why spots appear on plant leaves may be due to the lack of sugar, causing leaf tissues to starve and die. These sugars are commonly contained in saps, which these bugs extract from the leaves. Some of the sapsuckers that you may encounter are thrips, aphids, and spider mites.

2. Fungus

3.   Nutrient deficiency – if the root system of the plants appear to be brownish, then it is possible that your plants are suffering from nutrient deficiency. If the leaves also appear to be yellowing and the flowers fall after blooming, then it is a tell-tale sign that you need to check the nutrient solution that you are using.

4.   Phytotoxicity – rust-like flaws or aberrations on the leaves can be a sign that your plants have a negative reaction to the nutrition that they are taking in.

5.   Necrosis – check the EC meter on your reservoir and see if it is within range. The spots on the leaves may be an indication that the nutrient solution that you are using is too strong.

Treatment: Switch nutrient solution

While there are many factors that may contribute to the formation of aberration on leaves, you will realize that it is better to take a holistic approach and change the nutrient solution that you are using in the system altogether. It may be wise to switch back to commercial-grade nutrient solutions, or mix a fresh batch but with only half or ¾ of recommended strength. You may also want to add a bit of fungicide such as Fongarid to the nutrient solution. Do not add any additives – these may be causing toxicity in the nutrient solution. Before you add the new nutrient solution in your hydroponic system, make sure that you flush the roots with pH adjusted water to remove any possibly remaining toxic compound.

Check with hydroponic solution suppliers and ask for ingredients that are suitable for combatting root disease. Keep in mind that products that are available and suitable to use for this problem depend on the growth stage of your crop.

When you have already added a fresh solution, make sure that the water temperature stays in the range of 21-23 °C. After a week, replace the batch but do not add fungicide to rule out fungal infection. After 14 days, add preventive solutions such as friendly bacteria. If you are sure that fungus and bugs are the cause of the aberrations, you may want to spray your plants with fungicides and physically remove the bugs on the plants.

Leaves are Yellowing and Wilting

If you notice that the plant appears to be sick and the signs are appearing from the bottom of the plant, especially during the early flowering stage, then you may be dealing with root disease. Root disease happens when:

1. The plant is suffering from major nutrient deficiencies

2. The roots are being poisoned by the nutrient solution

3. The roots are suffering from Phytophthora, Pythium, or oxygen starvation.

Treatment: Check the nutrient solution you are using

To be safe, throw out the solution that you are currently using. Use a refill that only has half of the strength that you are using and then add a fungicide. After a week, dump the solution and add the same solution, but this time, without the fungicide. After a week, throw out the solution and add friendly bacteria. From here on, make sure that your solution contains friendly bacteria to combat root disease.

Make sure that the solution that you are using is below 25 °C or within the range of 20-23 °C. If your nutrient is not aerated, make sure that it is in the future so that the roots of your crops can also receive oxygen.

If you are using tap water treated with chlorine, then it is unlikely that your nutrient solution contains Pythium, a parasite that may dwell in your water source. If you are not using any water that passes through the soil, then you can also rule out Phytophthora, or a water parasite that are often found in any water source near the ground. At this point, you are sure that the root disease is caused by oxygen starvation. If you think that your hydroponic system is not allowing the roots to have access to oxygen, then you may consider changing the system altogether.

White Spots on the Leaves

White spots are mainly caused by the following:

1. Mildew or fungal formation on the leaves

2. Aphids, or tiny white bugs that appear collectively as white spots on the leaves

Treatment: Inspect the leaves with a magnifying glass and determine the cause of the spots

If you observe that the spots that you see are not due to the formation of bugs that may be feeding on the sap of your crops, then this is easily a fungi formation. Spraying fungicides is the best solution. On the other hand, if you see that the spots are aphid formations, spray commercial sap-sucking sprays such as Confidor. If your crops are already in the flowering stage, consider spraying organic-grade bug sprays instead.

Plants are too Big for the System

There are many reasons that this happens. When plants grow too big for the system and you are sure that they will be able to fit in the construction that you made, this may have happened because of the following reasons:

1.   The plants were switched down too late

2.   The plants may not be ideal for indoor growth

Treatment: Know the genetics of your plants and do artificial height controls

When plants are too big for your hydroponic system, it does not mean that you have to transfer all of them to larger hydroponic system. If your plants allow you to take cuttings and then move the removed parts to another system for cloning, then this may be the solution that is ideal for your problem. You may also use nets to control plant height and help you maintain a canopy level.

At the same time, it pays to know the genetics of the crops that you want to plant before you choose to grow them. For example, plants that are genetically known to have long equatorial growths are not suitable for indoor growth while short plant varieties with early flowering capacities may be the best choice for growing.

Leaves Appear as if Tips are Burned

When you see that the leaves of your crops look like the tips have burned or turned dark in color, it may be because:

1. The nutrient mix is too strong
2. There are salt buildups in the root system

Treatment: Take out the toxicity

When you observe these leaf burns, immediately flush the root system with pH adjusted water. Make sure that you throw out the nutrient solution that you are using and replace it with a very weak nutrient solution instead.

It is also very probable that the salt levels in your nutrient reservoir have changed. This happens when the plants take up more water and the rest of the nutrients compared to salts. The result is that the mixture left in the reservoir is too salty and consequently, toxic to your plants. You may want to calibrate your salt meter and check the amount of salts that are left in your reservoir every day to appropriately diagnose this problem. At the same time, follow the rule that your reservoir should be large enough to make sure that it still stores an adequate amount of water in the solution. That means that your tank should only be reduced by up to 20% only every cycle.

If you notice more severe leaf burning, then it is a sign that your reservoir is too small. Replace it with a bigger one immediately.

Leaves Curling Over

If you notice that the leaves of your plants appear to be curling over, then it is a sign that your nutrient solution has incorrect pH levels for your choice of crop. What happens here is that the plants are starving from certain nutrients, particularly Calcium. When you observe that the leaves of your plants are curling over, check the pH balance in your nutrient solution.

Leaves Curling Under

If you notice that the leaves of your plants behave this way, then it is very likely that you have over-fertilized your plants. If you are sure that the amount of water-soluble fertilizer is adequate for the nutrient solution that you are using, then check the pH balance of the solution and the EC meter to check if your plants are getting the right balance of nutrients.

Leaves Wilting

If the leaves of your plants are wilting, then your plants are likely suffering from excessive heat. Take note that most young plants are extremely fragile to heat exposure and may be sensitive to temperature. To check the amount of heat that your plants receive from the artificial lights that you may have installed, place a thermometer at plant height under the lights two hours after you have turned on your lamps. Check for the temperature as well three hours after you have turned off artificial lighting.

Leaves Turn into Purple Toward End of Flowering Stage

There are particular plant genetics that make it normal for leaves to turn to purple towards the end of flowering. If that is not part of your crop's genetics, then it is likely that your plants are suffering from Phosphorous deficiency, as plants do take up more Phosphorous as they mature. Increasing the pH levels to 6.1 to 6.2 may fix that deficiency.

Another factor that you may want to look at is the temperature that your plants receive during nighttime. It is possible that the temperature is extremely cold when the lights are off, and that the plants are shocked because of the sudden temperature change.

Flowers Rot

The most common culprit of flower rot is a fungal pathogen called Botrytis (commonly called among growers as Grey Mold). Take caution when this happens – once this pathogen grows into your crops, it may be almost impossible to contain it. If you notice this occurrence during the late flowering stage of your crop, then the solution is to pull out the crop as soon as you can. Botrytis spreads very quickly, and you may need to sacrifice some of your crops to save the rest. Also dump the remaining nutrient solution and flush the remaining crops with fresh water.

However, ensuring that your plants enjoy sufficient airflow is the best prevention against this pathogen. Also, including silica products also significantly reduces the likelihood that Botrytis will thrive in your crops in the future.

Plants Turning Yellow and Looking Sick

If this happens, check your light meters or the intervals of turning off and on of your lights. Keep in mind that when plants get excessive heat and light, it is possible for them to suffer from overheating.

If your light timers are fine and you know that your plants are getting sufficient heat and light, check on the roots of your plants. If they appear brown, then it is likely that they are suffering from potential root rot.

Flower Offshoots

If your plants have flower offshoots, then it is very possible that your plants are not getting the sleep that they need because light reaches them during nighttime. Plants need 12 hours of uninterrupted sleep for them to reach their full potential. Make sure that you do not have the habit of repeatedly checking your plants during lights off and that the light timers are working correctly.

If that is not the case, the culprit behind the offshoots will be excessive heat around the plants. Make sure that the room where your hydroponic system is located cools down adequately.

Temperature Around the Hydroponic System is Too High

High temperature is an enemy of any crop, and if you are using a hydroponic system for growing plants, it will be a bigger problem. The reason is because when the room where the system is gets too hot, the reservoir for your nutrient solution also gets hot, which may cause a number of problems for your crops. High air temperatures can cause some problems for your crops, so make sure that you do what it takes to lower the temperature in your room where your system is.

The best solution would be to make sure that your hydroponic system gets all the ventilation that it requires to maintain the required 28 °C that your plants need. If you find that your ambient room temperature at night is already at 32 °F, then you may find it difficult to lower the temperature during the day. The solution is to adapt a thermostat that will turn on exhaust fans when needed. It should be installed to monitor the temperature under the lights to monitor the temperature. If you still find the temperature still high, you may want to throw in some frozen water bottles in the nutrient solution to lower down the reservoir's temperature.

Yield Is Smaller than Usual

If the yields of your crops appear to be smaller than usual, this may be caused by different factors. However, the first thing that you should check will be the environment of your hydroponic system.

Among the primary causes of small crop yields is the age of the lamps that you are using. If you think that you have done all it takes to make your hydroponic system work, then look back at the last time that you replaced your lamps. The reason why this matters is this: while you think that your lamps are still burning brightly, the color spectrum that it emits drops significantly. Your lamps will be maintaining its color spectrum if it burns within 20,000 hours.

For this reason, it is advisable to replace your lamps every 10 months. For many growers, they make it a point to replace their lamps every third crop.

White Slime in the Reservoir

If you notice that there is a growth of white-colored slime in your nutrient tank, then you are witnessing the growth of bacteria. This should not be a problem if you know that the growth is a friendly bacteria (which you can even add to your nutrient solution to combat root rot); but if not, you may opt to check for the organism that is growing in your nutrient solution. As a preventive measure, you can use hydrogen peroxide; any sterilizing material can also prevent such growth.

Chapter Nine:
Cloning Your Hydroponic Plants

There are many growers who will want to stick to planting a particular plant and mass produce it. Since it is too troublesome to grow a plant from scratch, the best option to make sure that you are multiplying your crops quickly is to clone your hydroponic plant.

What is Cloning?

Cloning is simply the process of cutting a stem tissue or a leaf from a plant and then turning it into another plant. Because it is taken from a particular plant of your choice, you can be sure that the result of the clone will have all the desirable traits that you want in the new growth.

The idea of cloning is this: you, the grower, will only want plants that have all the desired qualities for ideal growth, which are already possessed by a hydroponic plant that you have successfully grown in a hydroponic system. This ensures you that you have a replica of that plant that will yield desirable crops as well.

The Principles of Cloning

Successful cloning is based on the following factors:

1.   Humidity

To create and cultivate a successful clone, it is best to cultivate the cutting in high humidity. This ensures that your clone will be able to absorb and maintain better moisture. Because moisture is present, you can be sure that your cutting will not be stressed, which will result in healthy and better strike rates.

If you grow a clone in an area with low humidity, you will see that the leaf clones are transpiring or losing moisture, which means that instead of absorbing water content, it instead gives out its own water into its environment. The result is obviously the drying out of your clone.

If it is not possible for you to have a room that has high humidity, you can use a propagator instead. A propagator is an enclosed unit complete with a transparent lid which serves as a controlled, humid environment for your clone.

2.   Oxygen and Moisture Ratio

Your first major goal in ensuring that you have a healthy clone is to encourage it to produce its own set of roots. However, you also want to make sure that the potential roots that are growing out of the clone will also absorb oxygen to prevent suffocation.

Most growers make the mistake of making the new growing medium (usually rockwool) too wet. This would, of course, drown the clone due to the lack of oxygen. If you want to use rockwool as the growing medium of your new clone, make sure that a 40x40 cube of rockwool weighs about 40 to 45 grams when moist.

3.   Temperature

Any good condition that encourages plant growth relies on the temperature of its growing media and environment air. This rule is also followed in cloning.

Like in your hydroponic system, the clone will suffer if the room temperature is too warm or too cold. For this reason, make sure that the air temperature where the clones are stays within 24 – 28 °C. To make sure that the temperature stays within this range, equip your clone's incubator with a thermostat.

Chapter Ten:
Enjoying the Yields

Now that you are capable of growing plants in a hydroponic system, it is time to ensure that the fruits of your hard labor are safe for you and your family to enjoy. Is it really safe to throw in the greens that you have been growing in your hydroponic system into the juicer right away?

Is Your Produce Dangerous?

According to many home hydroponic growers, people still need to take caution when it comes to consuming hydroponically-grown food. Many of the healthy food products that indoor growers produce, such as lettuce, herbs, salad greens, and wheatgrass, are included in the high-risk category of foodborne diseases. That is because most of these foods are consumed raw, with people veering away from the traditional way of killing bacteria, which is cooking.

Sadly, even the cleanest produce that you have created from a seedling at home can get contamination. Even the cleanest indoor garden can be a thriving spot for bacteria and pathogens if a grower is not aware of how easily he can spread them with his own tools or materials used for growing plants. For this reason, it is best to prevent getting the contamination onto your dinner table by knowing how crops can get contaminated and how it is possible for bacteria to thrive within the room that you are growing your crops in.

Crops are usually contaminated because of the following:

1. Incorrect use of compost for fertilizing

2. Use of contaminated tools

3. Unsanitary hydroponic systems

4. Toxic compounds found in nutrient solutions

5. Pest infestation

6. Unsanitary and improper human handling

Hydroponic Food Safety Rules

When you intend to produce plants in a hydroponic system for human consumption, it is best to observe the following rules:

1. If you plan to consume your produce raw, do not use any stabilized or composted manure as fertilizer, or any other animal compounds. If it cannot b helped, make sure that they are composted and packed in such a way that they are free of any bacteria.

2. Quality, clean water is a must for all hydroponic systems, since it is very possible for pathogens to thrive in untreated water.

3. Make sure that you wash your hands before you have contact with your plants. If you are using gloves, make sure that they are clean as well.

4. Try to prevent the edible portion of the plant from getting wet with the nutrient solution. Keep in mind that salad vegetables are very prone to contamination since they sit nearer to the water.

5. Keep your growing medium and area as clean as possible. Also, make sure that you remove any plants in your hydroponic solution that are suffering from irreparable root rot or sickness. Also, see to it that you remove old leaves, pruning remnants, and any organic material from a diseased plant.

6. Make sure that all the tools that are going to be used for harvest are clean. Handle all your hydroponic crops carefully to prevent them from bruising.

7. Run the harvested crops in running tap water instead of simply just soaking them in a basin. Bacteria spreads through washing water, and it's best to throw out the washing water as quickly as possible. If you are not going to consume the produce immediately, make sure that you place them in a container with a cover inside the refrigerator.

8. Dispose any vegetables or fruits that has already been cut if they are sitting for longer two hours in the counter at room temperature or if they have been out for longer an hour in a temperature that is higher than 90°F.

So long as you are following these rules for consuming hydroponically-produced crops, then you are sure that you are growing food in your home that is safe to eat. While making sure that your hydroponic system is sanitary dramatically reduces the danger of eating contaminated food, it still pays to prepare food with precaution. After all, you are already about to reap the fruits of your hard labor, so better make sure that everything that you have produced can truly be enjoyed!

Conclusion

Thank you once again for purchasing and reading this book.

I hope that you found it useful and enjoyable. By now you should have a pretty good grasp on the basics of hydroponic gardening methods and how they can help your plants grow faster, bigger and be more nutritious than what you are accustomed to from more traditional gardening methods.

The next step is to choose a few varieties of plant that you would like to grow and begin to construct your very own home hydroponic system. It is recommended that you start with the simple water culture method described in chapter three, as this method is easy enough to allow you to become familiar with the concepts of hydroponic gardening while not being too overwhelming for you at the beginning.

After you are familiar with the water culture method, you may wish to experiment with other, more complex methods. Your starter water culture system can easily be modified to the wick method by adding a second tank and a wick system. This is an excellent stepping stone to understanding more advanced and complicated systems and theories of soil-less growing. Mixing your own nutrient solution can be a fun project for those inclined to do so.

This is an optional step but learning about the process will have the by-product of deepening your understanding of hydroponics as a whole. You can decide for yourself if it's worth the trouble.

The possibilities are nearly endless when it comes to at home hydroponic systems. Designing and constructing your hydroponic system to your exact specifications so that works best with your situation and the crops you choose to grow is half of the fun.

When you set up your first system and grow your first few plants, you'll begin to see for yourself all the amazing benefits hydroponic gardening offers! What are you waiting for?

Good Luck and Happy Growing!

Mike

Other Related Books

Below are several links to books on Amazon.com related to the topic of Hydroponic Gardening. Enjoy!

Aquaponics: An Introduction to Aquaponic Gardening (3rd Edition)
http://goo.gl/FAPqzZ

Aquaponics: Creating Your Own Aquaponic Garden
http://goo.gl/06r8JH

Aquaponics: Aquaculture–An Introduction To Aquaculture For Small Farmers (3rd Edition)
http://goo.gl/XUdprR

Aquaponics 101: An Introduction To Backyard Aquaponic Gardening (2nd Edition)
http://goo.gl/TAf8M7

Hydroponics 101: A Complete Beginner's Guide to Hydroponic Gardening (3rd Edition)
http://goo.gl/26pFMP

An Introduction to Home Hydroponic Gardning (3rd Edition)
http://goo.gl/65c811

Photo Credits

89093731R00051

Made in the USA
Middletown, DE
13 September 2018